# Search Engine Optimization For The Local Business

by

Jim Hayne

**Legal Notices**

The information presented herein represents the view of the author as of the date of publication. Because of the rate with which conditions change, the author reserve the right to alter and update his opinion based on the new conditions. This book is for informational purposes only. While every attempt has been made to verify the information provided in this book, neither the authors nor their affiliates/partners assume any responsibility for errors, inaccuracies or omissions. Any slights of people or organizations are unintentional. You should be aware of any laws which govern business transactions or other business practices in your country and state. Any reference to any person or business whether living or dead is purely coincidental.

Every effort has been made to accurately represent this product and its potential. Examples in these materials are not to be interpreted as a promise or guarantee of earnings. Earning potential is entirely dependent on the person using our product, ideas and techniques. We do not purport this as a "get rich scheme."

Your level of success in attaining the results claimed in our materials depends on the time you devote to the program, ideas and techniques mentioned your finances, knowledge and various skills. Since these factors differ according to individuals, we cannot guarantee your success or income level. Nor are we responsible for any of your actions.

Any and all forward looking statements here or on any of our sales material are intended to express our opinion of earnings potential. Many factors will be important in determining your actual results and no guarantees are made that you will achieve results similar to ours or anybody else's, in fact no guarantees are made that you will achieve any results from our ideas and techniques in our material.

# Recommended Resources

Thanks for purchasing this book. Other books in this series can really help you grow your business. Especially <u>Getting Your Business In The Google 3-Pack: 25 Things You Need to Know</u>; <u>Online Reputation Management: 25 Things You Need to Know</u> and <u>How To Build An Optimized Website for Local Business: 25 Things You Should Know</u> for these topics go hand in hand with SEO for the local business.

# Table of Contents



Reviews online today are the driving force behind most of the purchases that are made, both online and in-store.

# About the Author

Jim Hayne is an American business marketing and sales specialist.  He lives in La Verne, California which is 40 miles east of Los Angeles.

Jim Has had three main careers in his life.  First, he had the opportunity to minister to young people as a youth minister for both Presbyterian and Baptist churches located mostly in Southern California.  Jim did this for over eighteen and a half years (you can tell he worked with youth when he emphasises the half year) before making a change to a new career in wealth management.   Working as a wealth manager, Jim helped both families and small business investors plan and invest toward their desired goals.  After seventeen plus years helping individuals with their money, Jim has helped many companies as a sales and marketing specialist.  Jim main focus is to move the needle in a positive direction for any person he works with.

Working in the wealth management arena, Jim was constantly approached by many so-called advertising specialist claiming they were the experts in delivering leads and he would have great success, if only he would invest in their system providing quality leads. One after another of these so called amazing lead systems failed miserably, and often delivered little or no results at all.   Realizing that success was really about getting new paying customers and clients through his door,   Jim began to grow his business by studying advertising and marketing and creating his own marketing of his design system.  Realizing that the old adage of sharpening the saw before cutting a tree really was important.

One thing you learn as a youth minister is that you do not wait for the young people to show up at the church, but you must visit the places the youth are located and build relationships there.  When Jim realized the solution to build his business was already answered in what he had been doing for almost two decades that put together a solution that worked.

Today, principals are the same, but methods may be a bit different due to technology.  Regular mail and postcards through the post office has been substituted by email.  Although mailings may have its usefulness because its stands out since so many do not use this method anymore.

Seminars have been replaced with webinars, and door knocking has been replaced with Facebook and other social media platforms.  Asking for referrals from friends have even been supplanted by Google, Yelp and Facebook and other online platforms.  Why the change?  Simple, we can save time and get more feedback by looking at the reviews scores and even dig deeper and read the reviews themselves.

The internet has changed the way we interact with one another and with our shopping.  Not all of the change is good, but most would agree it is the preferred method to interact with one another.   When we realize that currently Google is the number one source for research on just about anything, we know that Google is not going away anytime soon.  Most Americans use Google to find suggestions and recommendations for the services and products they desire.  Getting your business to be seen online is paramount to a successful business.

It is no different then having a nice looking storefront with a visable sign for new customers to find you on a physical street, as it is to have that same customer locate you online.  Having a quality website that is easy to find online is very important, just like having a business show in the Google 3 Pack would be in receiving new leads.

The quality of a businesses online presence can make or break financial success.  Having a quality website that actually helps draw in new customers/patients to your business, not just be an online business card, is paramount to success.

Having a website that communicates effectively by first being seen, and second conveying your message in a way that makes your website stand above your competition should be a focus for all businesses.  Having a quality website should never be taken lightly and sadly many small to mid sized business have never even created a website, much less upgraded from a slow and ineffectual site.

Having a website that is actually seen online is what this book is about.  Being found by using SEO (Search Engine Optimization) is actually more important than having a pretty website.  It is like a good looking car sitting in your driveway that is missing the engine, the vehicle will never work without the engine.  Website rarely brings new traffic if nobody is looking at it.

This is why this book is written, to help share insight and knowledge with small to mid sized businesses on how and why a quality website should be optimized using SEO techniques to help increase new paying customers.

Jim has been called the Google Ratings Guy because of his knowledge and expertise in helping businesses repair their online reputation and teaching how to get quality reviews in order to stand above your competition.  But having great reviews does little if your business is not found with online searches.

Having a quality website helps build your online presence and when created properly will deliver new paying customers through your business door.

You can contact Jim at smartadslocal@gmail.com for questions about SEO or any related topics.

# Introduction

The Internet was born about 25 years ago, and over the lifetime of the internet, this tool that has given our society many benefits, albeit both positive and negative.

It would be hard to imagine our world without the internet's time saving ability to learn about everything imaginable.  The internet is the access to a wealth of information – more than most people would ever know what to do with in a person's lifetime.

But while that diverse reach between all four corners of the world may be great for those simply looking for information, it can present a challenge for small businesses. The main question a small business owner should be asking is, "how do I use the internet to bring in new paying visitors into my business?"

But it does not have to be a challenge, in fact, it can be the best answer to helping your business gain many new customers every day.

Before the internet business had to advertise using print ads, telephone books, television ads, and radio. All forms of advertising had merit but was expensive. So only large corporations would be able to reach into the minds of people sitting at home to gain their interest into their products and services. Days of the mailbox being full of the print ads are gone, and I say thank goodness for that!

Yes, I know we still get some ads through letters and postcards, but the amount of such advertisements has decreased considerably. In fact, I remember looking through The Sears Catalog with large color print advertisements sent before Christmas. The investment on printing that large book filled with advertisement must have been incredible.

While huge corporations have the budget to reach around the globe and still gain customers, it's unlikely that the small mom-and-pop shop on a corner in Missouri is going to be able to do the same thing.

Even after the internet was born and telephone books, print ads, and other forms of advertisement have decreased, it is not easy for the average local business to gain exposure that the large corporations with tons of money have. Before Google algorithms and local SEO, this was a big problem. For the small business, a website or blog was simply a place to send customers to show them their business was legitimate and hopefully customers would spend a few moments on their website to to look at merchandise, get store information, or even possibly buy products.

But using the Internet and their website to gain new customers? It was unheard of.

Until now, over the last few years that has changed for the better for the local business owner.

With local SEO (Search Engine Optimization) the website or blog for that small business now becomes a place to attract new customers, gain new business, and drive sales and profits up. So, maybe that shop in Missouri still won't be able to deliver to a customer in China. What they will be able to do is pick up sales that are right outside their door, sales that they otherwise would never have even known of it wasn't for local SEO.

Businesses really need to master three key elements to having new customers visit their establishment. First, businesses need to be seen (SEO and advertising.) Second, businesses need to be credible (Reputation Management.) Third, business needs to build interest to visit (Website Design and using proper incentives.)

Using local SEO, a business can now be seen by their neighborhood, and gain so many new customers that prior to their SEO, would never see their location from the car or walking by the storefront. Being seen is really what Search Engine Optimization is all about. And you are now going to gain knowledge when put into use, to help your business prosper.

# What is Local SEO?

In order to answer this question, it first needs to be broken down.

SEO stands for "Search Engine Optimization." For business owners and webmasters, this means optimizing their search engine listings, website and webpages for the search engines. This ultimately means communication in the language search engines understand, to help the search engine put the people searching for your service, in front of your business information as well as website. Another term often used is driving traffic to your site.

When it comes to local SEO, the strategies and tactics used are very similar, with the exception that they are focused on optimizing *local* search. This means utilizing search engines like Google My Business and other directories, including local keywords, and ensuring that all content has a local focus.

By doing so, when customers hop online looking for a business in their area – something more and more customers are doing – they stumble upon the business listing and websites of a businesses that have what they need. But they'll only find those businesses that the search engine places in front of them, mainly because the business has taken the time to optimize (communicated their information in the fashion the search engines understand) their online content for local SEO.

At its core, local SEO is simply a form of advertising, and once businesses start seeing it that way, they quickly see how important it is.

Local SEO is an extremely targeted form of advertising because the business owner isn't actually advertising directly to the customer. The best analogy is like telling your friend, to tell another friend who has interest in what your selling to give you a call.

It's this way that local SEO is <u>unlike</u> television commercials, print ads, and brochures. While these methods may fall upon the ears of hundreds or even thousands, and only get the business one or two new customers, local SEO isn't blanket advertising. Business owners don't just have to put it out there and hope for the best.

By its very nature, local SEO automatically <u>targets a specific audience.</u> And, because the information is delivered to the targeted group, it's even cheaper than all of those traditional forms of advertising put together.

# How Searches Work

In order to understand SEO of any kind, including local SEO, you must first understand the basics of how Google works. Of course there are other search engines involved in search as well, but Google isn't just the biggest search engine, it's also considered the gold standard when it comes to SEO.

Constant new information is being created online every single second. A new video is being uploaded, a new blog post, or a new webpage, to name just a few types of online activity. In order to find this information in the seconds it takes Google to pull up a search results page, the search engine needed to come up with a way to quickly organize the pages and find the most relevant to display.

When Google created a way to do it, it was a fairly complicated nameless algorithm; people often referred to it as "Google's spiders". In 2013 however, Google overhauled and simplified that algorithm. They also gave it a name that it still uses today – Hummingbird.

The Hummingbird algorithm is made up of many different parts, very much the same way a computer is made up of different parts that all help it run and perform. Google regularly releases new parts that have been added to the algorithm including Panda, Penguin, Mobile Friendly, and Pigeon – the part of the algorithm designed to improve local results.

There are certain signals the algorithm, and all the many parts of it, look for when searching for websites to display in their search results after a user has made a query. Two of the most important signals are words and links.

PageRank – most often just called page rank - is another part of the Hummingbird algorithm, and a very important feature when it comes to local SEO as it deals with links specifically. Page rank determines how many other webpages point to one website, or one webpage. Every link is counted as a vote for the webpage it links to, and each vote will increase a website's page rank, getting them to rank higher in the search engine.

Words are also easily one of the most important signals the algorithm will look for. In SEO terms, these are known as 'keywords', and they are crucial. The keywords are the words someone will enter into Google when looking for a particular product or service. So, if someone was looking for a mortgage broker, they might enter the term "mortgage broker" into the search field. At their most basic, this is how words signal to the algorithm what the webpage is about.

Once a business owner understands *how* Google works, they can then learn to work *with* it, and post content that will direct Google – and therefore, users – to their website and to their business.

This is local SEO, and there are a number of best practices to follow in order to make the best use of it.

# The 18 Best Practices for Local SEO

Once you understand how searches work in relation to local SEO, it is time to start putting that knowledge to use. As mentioned, there are a number of practices that can further a business' local SEO efforts.

Business owners can choose to do as many or as little of these as they choose, but to really make the most of an online presence and brand, it's best that they're all done. The problem is that business owners are often busy running their business and so don't have the time to do all of it on their own. This is where a local SEO consultant can help, and there are always a number of them available. These specialists you'll find very easy with a quick Google search, as they truly know how to make the best of it!

Even business owners that work with a consultant however, still need to have a basic understanding of how local SEO works and the strategies used. This can help ensure that all work that's done within local SEO will still represent the voice of the business and the brand.

## Best Practice #1 – Create a Google My Business Listing

Google My Business, formerly known as Google Places, has become the starting point for all successful local SEO campaigns.

Google My Business is the foundation of local listings and without it, a business' name will not show up in the local listings. These listings are already becoming more competitive. While Google used to include a "7 pack" of local businesses, they have dwindled that down to just three since most people now use their smartphones, so only the top three businesses are shown in full. The only way for a business to give themselves the best chance to appear there is by creating a Google My Business listing.

Setting up a Google My Business listing isn't very difficult and will take just a couple of minutes. Business owners should visit www.google.com/business to get started, click on the 'Start Now' button and follow the subsequent instructions.

Google gives business owners the option of filling out as much or as little information as they'd like, but it's most recommended that as much information as possible is provided. Other tips to follow when creating a Google My Business listing is:

- Choose a profile picture that is intriguing to users and is relevant to the business.
- While the picture is important, the title of the image file is also important. It should include a keyword, which could be the business' location, name, or phone number.
- Multiple images not only give users better insight into the business, they can also give Google more keywords. Several pictures (a minimum of 12) should be uploaded, with each having its own relevant keywords.
- Categories are one of the fields Google will search first when users are searching for a particular type of business. Because of this, business owners must carefully choose a category for their Google My Business listing.

- Multiple categories can be chosen, but Google recommends keeping it to one or two, if possible.
- Once a Google My Business listing is published, the exact name, address and phone number of the business needs to be written down exactly as it's shown on the listing. Other listings are likely to be created in the future, and it's crucial that all listings remain consistent.

Best Practice #2 – Create Other Business Listings

Google My Business might be the gold standard of local SEO, but there are other online directories that business owners should also utilize. They operate in a very similar way that Google My Business does, and each only takes a few minutes to create. Having as many listings as possible across multiple directories will give business owners a bigger online presence and can help further promote the brand.

The top online directories every business should appear on are:

- Yahoo! Aabaco Small Business
- Bing Places for Business
- Yelp for Business Owners
- MerchantCircle
- Superpages.com
- CitySearch
- Mapquest/Yext
- Local.com
- Foursquare
- LinkedIn
- Angie's List

- Manta
- Kudzu

# Best Practice #3 – Keyword Research

Once a business appears across all online directories,
they will have already increased their page ranking for
certain keywords. Keywords play a huge part of local
SEO. These are the words users enter into search
engines when they're looking for a particular service,
product, or information. Google uses those words and
searches across pages online to deliver the most
relevant results to the user.

The goal for businesses looking to succeed in their
local SEO efforts need to do a bit of research on these
keywords. While some keywords, such as 'plumber'
for a plumbing business are going to be obvious, others
won't be. And business owners that don't perform

keyword research will miss out on some that could be very valuable to them.

Google is the authoritative voice when it comes to SEO of any kind, so it makes sense that they would also offer the gold standard in terms of keyword research tools.

Google Keyword Planner is free to use, and it's also one of the best keyword research tools available. Google Keyword Planner tells website owners how many people are searching for keywords that are relevant to their business. The tool will also break this amount down into a monthly account. This can be especially helpful for owners of seasonal businesses that may offer different products or services during different times of the year.

The Planner can be accessed through any Google AdWords account. Any business that has a website or blog likely has a Google AdWords account. If not, one should be created by going to http://adwords.google.com. Once an account is created, the Google Keyword Planner tool can be accessed by

logging into
http://adwords.google.com/KeywordPlanner.

Once logged into the Keyword Planner, keywords can be found by entering the website's landing page, business category, and product or service the business offers under 'Find new keywords'. This is where business owners can enter the obvious keywords for their business such as 'plumber' or 'florist' or other relevant terms.

This is what SEO consultants do with general SEO, but with local SEO it needs to be taken a step further. Google defaults the country targeting field to 'Anywhere.' But when local SEO is a focus, it should be changed to a specific geographical location, such as 'plumbers New York City'. After entering these terms and clicking 'Get Ideas,' a list of keywords will be generated.

The Google Keyword Planner is just one tool that's available to help business owners generate keywords. There are many more out there, and while some do have a small fee attached, it can be worthwhile when quality keywords are delivered.

Some of the best keyword research tools available are:

- o <u>Semrush</u>
- o <u>Long Tail Pro</u>
- o <u>SE Cockpit</u>
- o <u>WordTracker</u>

Best Practice #4 – Creating Keywords

With a list of generated keywords in hand, any business owner will be well on their way to improving their SEO efforts. However, the keywords provided by the research tools aren't enough if they don't include local keywords and long-tail keywords.

Many people think that using local keywords is simply attaching the name of the city or state at the end of a keyword. That's partly true, but just like the keyword 'plumber' can generate dozens of keywords, so can locations.

For instance, local keywords for the term 'plumber' could include 'New York plumber', 'Plumber in New York', 'Plumber near New York', and more.

When using local keywords, business owners make it much easier for local people to actually find their business, and use it. These keywords aren't typically used so much for the search engines, as they are the people that are using them.

The opposite is true for long-tail keywords. Long-tail keywords are keywords that make up a phrase of about

5 or more words. Google and the other search engines love long-tail keywords because they best reflect the user's intent; they tell the search engine exactly what the user is looking for. Like local keywords, long tail keywords have a lower search volume, but they do have a much higher conversion rate than head, or standard, keywords.

In addition to local and long-tail keywords, keyword modifiers can also be used. These come in the form of adjectives or secondary products and services.

When using adjectives as keyword modifiers, they can be anything from 'best' to 'cheap' or 'affordable'. These are terms that users often use when searching for a business because they'll likely be spending money there, and they want to make sure they're using the best business to get the most value for their money.

Secondary services the business offers are also considered to be keyword modifiers. In the case of the plumber, this might include keywords such as 'plumbing repair' or 'commercial plumbers.'

Using keyword modifiers won't only broaden the list of keywords available, combining them with local keywords will also give business owners great long-tail keywords.

Best Practice #5 – Analyze Keywords

Once a list of keywords has been generated, they then need to be analyzed. This isn't something that all businesses do, but they should, as it will show which keywords are still quite relevant, and which are starting to fall in popularity.

Google once again, is on top of this. Using Google Trends, found at https://www.google.com/trends/, keywords can be entered and business owners can see which keywords are searched for most often. Even more, Google Trends will also break down this volume into specific areas, making it a huge asset to those focused on local SEO.

Of course, while Google might be the first go-to for many webmasters, there are others out there to try, and just like Google, they're largely free. They include:

- o SEO Book
- o Web SEO Analytics
- o Internet Marketing Ninjas

Best Practice #6 – Create Great Title Tags

Once all the research has been done, the next steps to improve local SEO actually happen on the page, and it all starts with the title tag.

A title tag is the title that's shown in the search engines as the title of the webpage. It also appears at the top of the browser of any webpage. And when it comes to content, the search engine algorithms place a lot of importance on them, as they really give the robots and algorithms an idea of the context of the webpage's content.

But what makes a great title tag?

- o   They are less than 55 characters.

- o The business' name is clearly visible.
- o They include one primary keyword that has high volume and is highly relevant to the business.
- o Use keywords close to the beginning of the title tag, if possible.
- o Title tags should be unique, with each webpage having its own title tag.
- o When focusing on local SEO, the geographic location should also appear in title tags.

Best Practice #7 – Create Great Meta Descriptions

After the title tag, the next aspect of any webpage the robots will search through is the meta description. The meta description are the one or two lines that appear underneath a page's title in the search engine result pages. Like title tags, meta descriptions appeal not only to the search engine robots, but also to readers who are looking for interesting information.

Also like title tags, there are tips business owners can follow to make sure they're creating great meta descriptions.

- o They should contain important keywords relevant to the business, and that have a high search volume.
- o Each meta description should be unique, just as title tags should.
- o Each page within a website should be optimized for different keywords.
- o Users will also see the meta description, so it's important that it's engaging and entices them to click onto that webpage.

o   Like title tags, for local SEO purposes, the geographic location should also be included in meta descriptions.

Best Practice #8 – Optimize Images

Optimizing images is important for a couple of reasons. The first is that image files are by their very nature, much larger than text files and therefore, take much longer to load. However, Google and the other search engines now consider the loading speed of a website when ranking pages, and they'll place slower-loading pages further down in the search results page.

But while the search engines may realize that a webpage has a file on it that will take longer to load, they cannot read or understand image files. So when there is an image on a page, the search engines only know that it's an image file; they don't understand what the image is actually of. This is another reason why image files need to be optimized.

Luckily, there are a few ways to optimize images so that the search engines can better load, and better understand them.

- o Resize images to the smallest file size possible, without affecting the quality of the image.
- o Inserting 'Alt Text' code to each image when it's uploaded to the website will tell the search

engine what the picture is of. This way they'll be able to identify and understand the image, and rank the page appropriately. Adding 'Alt Text' code to images is different for every blogging and website creation program and platform, but it's generally very easy across the board.

o Name all images that are uploaded to the website, and be sure that their names include relevant keywords. This will help the search engines understand what the image is about.

o Give all image file names on one website have a unique name.

o While it may seem odd to attach a geographic location to an image file, it's important to do so, as it will tell the search engines even more about the file.

Better Practice #9 – Optimize Anchor Text

Anchor text isn't something that webmasters and business owners have complete control of, but they can optimize it to work in their favor.

Anchor text is the text that is used when one website links to another website, otherwise known as backlinks. Business owners want anchor text linking to their website that is relevant to their business, so keywords such as "plumbers in New York" or "plumbers near New York."

While anchor text isn't completely within the control of the business owner, anchor text is also included within an actual website, when one page links to another. This is an area where business owners can truly optimize their own anchor text, as it helps the search engines understand the keywords business owners use to describe their own page.

While you might not be able to fully control the quality or quantity of backlinks, business owners can analyze and track their backlinks through a number of resources. The most commonly used are:

- Ahrefs
- Linkody
- Cognitive SEO
- Kerboo
- Link Research Tools

Best Practice #10 – Go Mobile

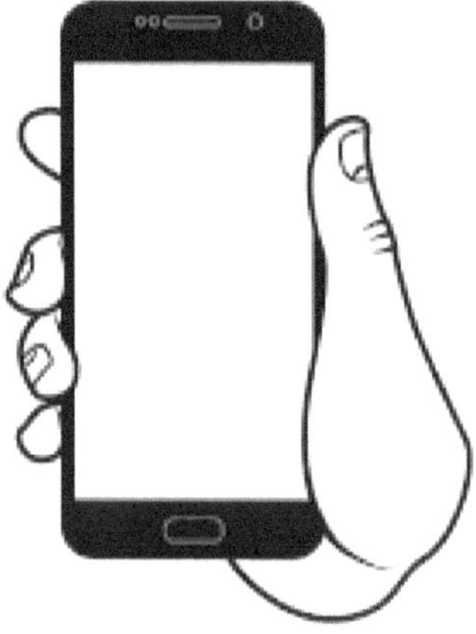

Mobile, mobile, mobile – it can't be said enough. If business owners want to improve their local SEO, they must ensure that their website is mobile-friendly; there's just no way around it.

In one of their latest updates, Google announced that that they had focused on mobility, and that sites that weren't 100% compliant with the new mobile requirements would be penalized. And that those penalizations would come in the form of those websites being placed lower down on the search engine results page.

To check to see how Google looks at your website, go to this url https://search.google.com/test/mobile-friendly and type in your url into the search bar.  This will give you a report from Google on your website and if it meets their requirements for mobile optimization.  If you realize that Google is not passing your website for mobile optimization, then it may be time to get a new website designer. If your website was created by a family member or friend, this may be the time to realize the actual cost of losing new paying customers because your website is not optimized intermally.  Worse, if you have a website development team, and you pay for their monthly service, and you have not had the team bring up the lack of optimization to you, it is time to fire your website team.

Best Practice #11 – Create Tags for Headings and Sub-Headings

Using headings and sub-headings on a website is another great way to grab the attention of the search engines. These again, give the search engines an indication of the context of the webpage, but it helps if the headings and sub-headings are tagged.

Headings are the most important, and there's typically only one on each page. These should be given an "H1" tag, which will tell the search engines that text is for the main heading on the page. Sub-headings can be given tags as well, and these are typically "H2", "H3", and so on as needed for each subsequent sub-heading.

Of course, wherever there is text within a webpage, there are also keywords and this includes headings of all kinds. The most important, or most relevant, keyword should be included within the "H1" tag. And when it comes to local SEO, the most important keywords should include the geographic location of the business.

Best Practice #12 – Optimize URL Structure

The URL is the address that can be seen in the browser and it indicates the webpage that a user is visiting. URLs are often overlooked by business owners when performing SEO, but they can be very important.

For instance, the following URL: www.aaaplumbers.com will tell visitors and search engines that the webpage most likely falls under the plumbing category. However, this URL: www.aaaplumbers.com/plumbing-services/newyork tells users and search engines so much more about the page, and the company.

Like meta descriptions, optimizing URL structure is something that is done within website creation platforms and programs, so each will be slightly different. However in most cases, it's not difficult and will take just minutes to do.

Best Practice #13 – Using Schema

Schema.org has revolutionized the way search engines display websites in their results pages. Schema is a markup code that can be placed on any website to allow search engines to give more information to the user. This information can include things like online reviews, prices, sitelinks, number of hours, and even entire menus right within the search results.

Not only does Schema help the search engine robots, which will in turn increase a website's page ranking, it also helps users and thereby can increase the click-through rate.

Because Schema gives the users so much more information, they tend to click on more websites that have included Schema because they know so much more about it. This can increase a site's CTR (click-through rate), which will also increase a website's page ranking.

To include Schema markup code on a website, visit schema.org and click on 'get started!' The schema markups that local businesses tend to make the most use of are:

- <u>Local Business Schema and Geotag</u>
- <u>Review</u>
- <u>Events</u>
- <u>Coupons and offers</u>
- <u>Videos</u>
- <u>Persons, individuals and employees</u>
- <u>Products</u>
- <u>City</u>

Best Practice #14 – Increase Local Citations

Citations in the local SEO world are any mentions of a local business on other websites. In order to be considered an actual citation however, the name, address and phone number must all be included. This is known as 'NAP'. The search engines love citations, even when there is no backlink to accompany them.

Often business owners make the mistake of thinking that just like anchor text, they have no control over the number of citations for their business online. However, this is not true. One of the best ways to get citations is to create profiles across all of the online directories mentioned in Best Practices 1 and 2. Because these will all include the NAP for the business, each will be considered an individual citation.

The best places to get or create citations are:

- Third-party websites, such as online directories
- Local blogs
- Industry-focused directories
- Industry-focused blogs
- Citations from competitors

Best Practice #15 – Get Positive Online Reviews

Reviews online today are the driving force behind most of the purchases that are made, both online and in-store. More than ever people are researching products and businesses before they use them, and having no reviews online can be just as bad as having negative reviews out there. Since I have written a book on this subject **Online Reputation Management: 25 Things You Need to Know**, you should know that this is an important topic.

In order to get reviews, all business owners have to do is ask their customers. Ask them to visit review sites such as Google, TripAdvisor or Yelp and leave positive reviews. For some reason, in my practice, I have to train staff to ask for reviews.  It seems that many believe that it is an uncomfortable process, and one that may have people say "no."  The truth is, it can be very fun, even when you get the "no's" shared as long as you are professional and have fun asking.

Just think of the review being worth $100 to your business, because it is at least that important.  Every positive review will help many people decide to visit your establishment over another competitor.  To have a great review score you need to remember 5 key elements.  1) Have a 4.7 – 4.9 score.  2) Have at least 100 more reviews then your closest competition. 3) Get good content in the reviews, not just the 5 star rating, but have the customer say why they gave you 5 stars. 4) Have recent reviews, when a business has a good score, but not a had a new review in many months or longer, people wonder if something has changed and search engines want to see regular postings as part of their reward system.  5) Responses to the reviews. Every review given to a business is a point in the eyes of the search engines, you can add points by responding to the reviews with a kind thank you.

Also make sure that this is a consistent effort. Having a few reviews online just isn't enough. Business owners need to continuously make sure new positive reviews are being added all the time, both to keep them up to date for users, and to keep the search engines happy.

Some tips to help businesses increase the amount of positive online reviews they receive are:

- o Make it easy by including "Find us on Google/Yelp" banners on the business' website.

- o Place direct links to review websites within different areas of the business' website and/or in email signatures.
- o Send thank you cards, and ask for a review by including a link in the card.
- o Offer an incentive, such as a monthly draw for all reviewers, to entice people to leave reviews.
- o Be sure to always thank reviewers.

Best Practice #16 – Creating Social Media Profiles

Social media has a huge influence on local SEO for a number of reasons. One is that it lets a business claim more of their business' name and brand online. There may be lots of "AAA Plumbers" or even "AAA Plumbers NY", and the first business that claims that name across Facebook, Twitter, Instagram, and other social media platforms will have the advantage in building that brand and image.

Social media is also a great way to get reviews and citations that are mentioned above. Every time someone mentions a business on Twitter, their followers can see it and your followers can see it. And if that mention gets a retweet or two, the number of people seeing that tweet about that business can quickly escalate into the thousands.

Social media also lets business owners interact directly with their customers, which is another reason it's a great boost to local SEO. Business owners can tweet about their upcoming promotion, or upload photos of their newest products. This will drive in the business that's right around the corner of a local business, and that's what local SEO is all about.

The biggest social media platforms businesses should be on are:

- o Facebook
- o Twitter
- o Instagram
- o Tumblr
- o LinkedIn
- o Google+

Best Practice #17 – Track, Track, Track

Once all of the SEO and local SEO work has been done on a website, the last thing a business owner should do is leave it to run on its own and hope for the best. Algorithms for Google and the other search engines are always changing, certain keywords trend more than others at different times, and things are always changing. Business owners that don't keep up with those changes regularly will be left to eventually, do all the local SEO work all over again.

And this is an area once again, where Google has provided an answer, and it's in the form of Google Analytics.

Google Analytics, which can be found at http://analytics.google.com, is a tool that can be used to track every activity that happens when users visit your site – and it's completely free to use. Once an account is created and Google has started to track conversion rates and other aspects of the website, it takes about 24 hours for a website's stats to appear. After that it will track continually, and users can look at it any time of the day to see what their website has been doing for the past hour, day, week, or month.

Best Practice #18 – Audit Competitors

Every business wants know how their competitors doing, and especially, how they are doing in relation to the owner's business. They may visit the store, inquire among mutual customers, and generally keep an open ear for news about their competitors. But, a business can audit the local SEO efforts of their competitors as well to see how they stack up, where they can improve, and where they have an edge over the competition.

Performing local SEO audits on competitors isn't difficult, although it can take quite a bit of time. In reality, it's just checking all the same steps and Best Practices that have been mentioned, but tracking them for the competitor. This may involve checking out their Twitter profile, or their Google My Business listing. A quick search of the competitor's name in Google will bring up relevant results, as will searching for reviews and citations.

Auditing the local SEO efforts of competitors is important because, just like all other areas of business, it can help one see where in relation their business stands.

# Conclusion

Many business owners mistakenly believe that local SEO efforts are highly technical, and that they require an in-depth knowledge only held by the most well-trained IT experts.

This simply isn't true.

Implementing local SEO strategies does take time, and it certainly is a bit of effort. But it's also something that every single business can do, and it doesn't require a great deal of technical knowledge.

Still, finding the time to dedicate to implementing those strategies can be difficult, as business owners are generally very busy running their busy. For these individuals, a local SEO or marketing consultant can help take care of all a business' local SEO requirements, and helping them realize the successes they've always been dreaming of.

However business owners choose to do it, there's no doubt – and study after study has proven it – local searches are increasing. And when businesses can keep up with those trends, and make it easier for local people to find them, they can use those searches to their advantage. They can use them to actually increase their customer base, and increase their bottom line.

If you are interested in having my business help you, I would be honored and will give you a discount by simply telling me you read this book.  Simply email me at smartadslocal@gmail.com and let me give you a great deal to help your business bring in more paying guests.

If you need some other marketing help, visit DFYbusinessinabox.com.  For a great package that will include a website, logo, Facebook banner and posts, business cards, and more.  When checking out on the website, you can contact the owner and mention that you read this book, you will get an extra discount on top of their great package deal.

# Next Steps

Ready to prosper?  I can only hope that this was not a book that gets placed on a table and forgotten, but is really a help to your business.  It amazes me to see so many wonderful business close their doors, not because they had a bad product or price, but because people did not see them online.  Don't be that business!  Please, implement the steps outlined in this book, and when traffic begins to pour into your business, please send me an update at smartadslocal@gmail.com  I would be honored.

www.ingramcontent.com/pod-product-compliance
Lightning Source LLC
Chambersburg PA
CBHW051233250726
48655CB00006B/2740